I HAVE A
CLEAR AND
FOCUSED MIND.

I AM AN
UNSTOPPABLE
FORCE OF
NATURE

I BELIEVE IN MYSELF.

I SET GOALS AND GO AFTER THEM WITH DETERMINATION.

I AM IN CONTROL OF MY THOUGHTS AND EMOTIONS.

I TELL THE DAY WHAT IT WILL BE.

I LIVE MY LIFE
WITH
INTENTION.

I AM IN
CONTROL OF
MY TIME.

I RELEASE THINGS THAT DO NOT SERVE MY HIGHEST SELF.

MY SKILLS AND TALENTS OPEN DOORS FOR ME.

I AM GETTING
BETTER AND
BETTER
EVERY DAY.

I GO GET
WHATEVER
I WANT.

IF I DESIRE SOMETHING, I OBTAIN IT.

I KNOW MY
POWER.

TODAY IS A
PHENOMENAL
DAY.

ABUNDANCE
FINDS ME
EVERYWHERE I
GO.

I TRUST THAT ALL THINGS ARE WORKING FOR GOOD.

I WAKE UP
MOTIVATED.

I CAN BE
WHATEVER I
WANT TO BE.

I CAN BE
WHATEVER I
WANT TO BE.

I AM A LIVING,
BREATHING
EXAMPLE OF
MOTIVATION.

I AM
ACHIEVING
GOALS, ONE
AT A TIME.

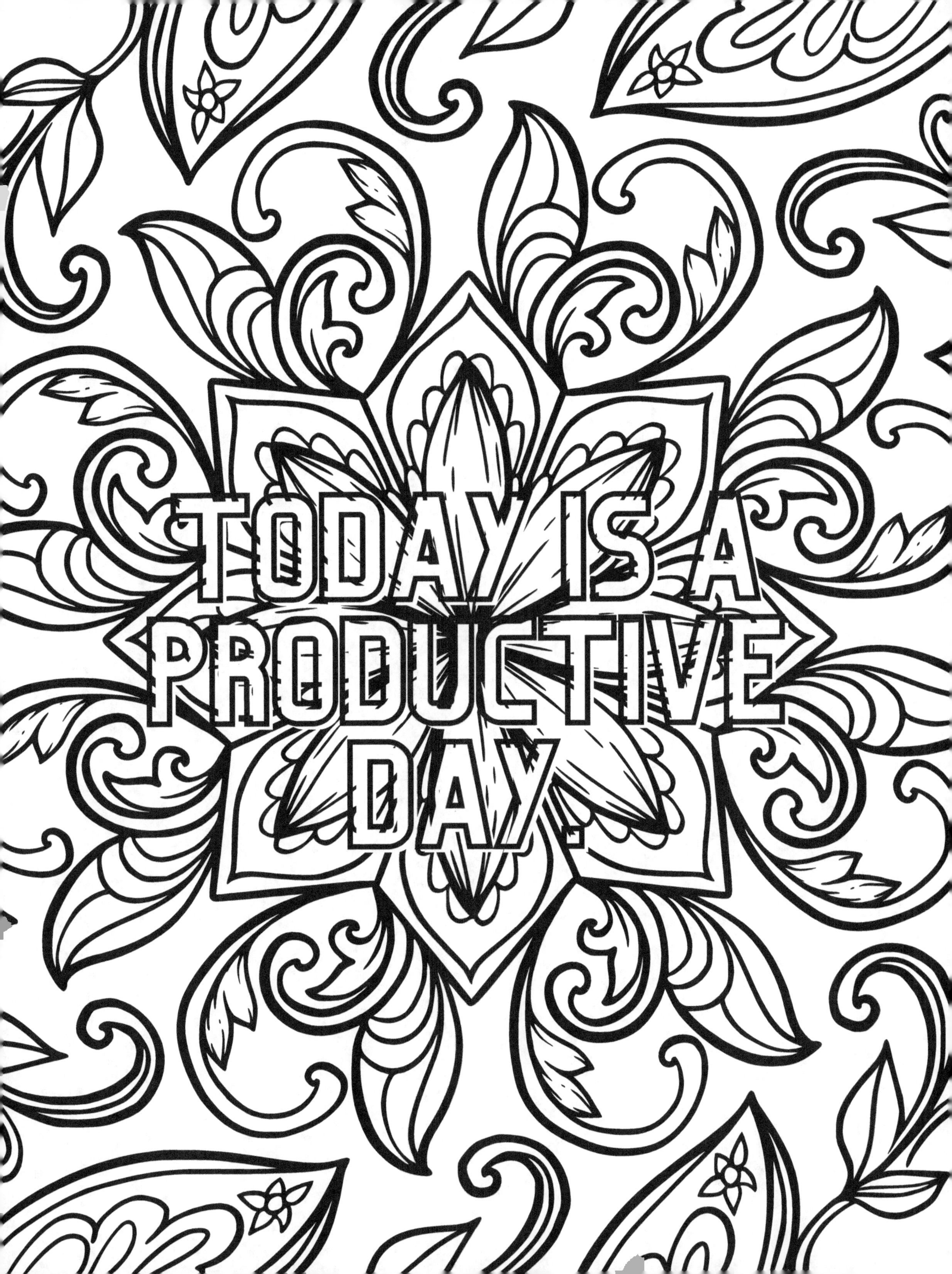

TODAY IS A
PRODUCTIVE
DAY

I UNDERSTAND
THAT NO
DREAM IS TOO
BIG.

I MOTIVATE OTHERS.

I MOVE WITH GRACE AND AUTHORITY.

TODAY IS A
PRODUCTIVE
DAY.

I UNDERSTAND
THE POWER OF
MY TONGUE.

I SPEAK LIFE.

9 798373 042468